People of the Middle Ages

Pilgrim

Melinda Lilly

Original illustrations by Cheryl Goettmoeller and Patti Rule

Rourke

Publishing LLC
Vero Beach, Florida 32964

www.rourkepublishing.com

For Bruce

PICTURE CREDITS: Page 5, MS. Canon. Ital. 74, fol. 73, courtesy of the Bodleian Library, University of Oxford; Page 9, MS. Douce 331, fol. 52, courtesy of the Bodleian Library, University of Oxford; Page 10, MS. Rawl. poet. 224, fol. 1, courtesy of the Bodleian Library, University of Oxford; Page 18, Arrival of Saint Ursula at Cologne (1280–1348), by Bernardo Daddi, altarpiece, painted about 1333, 60 x 63 cm., The J. Paul Getty Museum, Los Angeles; Page 21, MS. Douce 300, fol. 66, courtesy of the Bodleian Library, University of Oxford; Page 26, "Saint Bellinus Celebrating Mass," from the Gualenghi-d'Este Hours, by Taddeo Crivelli and Guglielmo Giraldi (illuminators), illuminated about 1469, 10.8 x 7.9 cm., The J. Paul Getty Museum, Los Angeles. Cover illustration and original art on pages 6, 13, 17, and 29 by Cheryl Goettemoeller; Original art on pages 14, 22, and 25 is by Patti Rule.

Cover illustration: Two pilgrims on their travels. In the Middle Ages (years 500 to 1500) people from many religions and backgrounds, including kings and poor people, were pilgrims.

Editor: Frank Sloan

Cover design by Nicola Stratford

Library of Congress Cataloging-in-Publication Data

Lilly, Melinda
    Pilgrim / Melinda Lilly
      p. cm. — (People of the middle ages)
    Includes bibliographical references and index.
    Summary: Introduces the way of life of the Christian pilgrim of the Middle Ages, looking at the foods one might have eaten, sights visited, and objects sought along the way.
      ISBN 1-58952-230-3
      1. Christian pilgrims and pilgrimages—Juvenile literature. 2. Middle Ages—Juvenile literature. 3. Civilization, Medieval—Juvenile literature. [1. Pilgrims and pilgrimages. 2. Religious life. 3. Middle Ages. 4. Civilization, Medieval.] I. Title II. Series.

BX2323 .L55 2002   2001056513
263' .042'0902—dc21

Printed in the USA

CG/CG

Table of Contents

Take a Trip

Do you like to take trips? If you lived in Europe 800 years ago, you might have been a **pilgrim**. You would have taken trips to holy places. In the **Middle Ages** (from the year 500 to 1500) many people were pilgrims.

You might walk hundreds of miles to see shoes once worn by a holy man. You hope the sight will make you a better person.

A picture of Mount Sinai, a holy place of the Middle East. Pilgrims traveled to the top of the mountain. This picture is from a book made by hand in the Middle Ages.

Tralauisla ebaniti apunto inmedio
e toppon porto della terra sancta
che dicolui tonerethe esser predio
che capo de xpiam esser sinanta
ton equel regno re tenne suo sedio
che facia lopra che ogni di si canta
one elsco sepulcro di vhu
laroue cruasfisso p noy su...

Jonequesto ecapo di guivea
nerso lenante unprovua esta mano
eda sinistra mano egalilea
edalponente esta elsume gioroano
e camaria segue caesaria
caca esur esaterta elibano
monte ouoe escie elsume diduo fonti
qin tecnnella caltri sammonti.

Traffic Jam of the Middle Ages!

It's the year 1300. You decide to visit churches in Rome. You're not the only one. More than half a million people join you. Paths and roads in Rome are jammed!

Who goes on these trips? People of many religions and everyone from kings to poor people are pilgrims. However, most pilgrims of Europe are Christians.

Pilgrims cross the Swiss Alps in the summertime.

Why Do You Want to Be a Pilgrim?

Perhaps the goal of your trip is to pray for a miracle. You might want to win a battle or become healthy if you are sick. One man urged his sister Margery to pray for a husband!

Too busy to go? Pay someone to go in your place.

If you break the law, you can be forced to be a pilgrim. The trip is your punishment. Metal chains weigh you down as you trudge to forgiveness.

A pilgrim begins her journey. Pilgrims usually traveled in a group.

9

Relics

You may hope to see a **relic**. It is a bone or other part of a dead holy person. It can also be something once touched by someone holy.

Many people of the time think that relics work miracles. Some believe that they bless you when you look at them. For this reason, churches keep them in cases with clear glass windows. This clear glass was used to make the first eyeglasses in 1285.

These pictures tell the story of the holy tear, a relic. Upper left: The holy tear. Upper right: The knight gets the relic. Lower left: Carrying the relic. Lower right: Delivering it.

Where in the World Do You Go?

Pilgrim, how do you decide where to go? In Rome, you can see the cloth believed to have wiped Jesus' face as he carried the cross. Some think that seeing it will bring blessings for 12,000 years.

Want to get away? A trip to holy places in the Middle East takes many months.

How about England? You can follow in the footsteps of the famous characters of *The Canterbury Tales,* by Geoffrey Chaucer. Most of them were pilgrims heading to Canterbury, England.

Pilgrims arrive at Canterbury Cathedral.

Planning Your Trip

There are many things to do to get ready! If you are married and English, you first must ask your wife or husband's permission. The answer is yes? Good. Now, read the guidebooks and choose people to travel with you.

Finally, it's time to pack. The pilgrim uniform is a long, hooded gray robe, a hat, hose, and comfortable shoes. Remember to bring a purse (called a **scrip**) to hold your belongings, a water bottle, and a walking stick.

A pilgrim leaves for his trip.

15

What a Blessing!

You need your priest's blessing before you leave for your trip. When you enter the church, lie down in front of the altar and pray. Listen as the choir sings for you. After you get up, the priest sprinkles your scrip and walking stick with holy water.

At the end of the church service, you receive a certificate that proves you are a pilgrim. Anyone who sees it will know you are not a spy or beggar.

The blessing of the scrips and walking sticks

Sleep Tight!

You and your group set off singing. Tonight, perhaps you'll sleep in England's Great Bed of Ware. It's the biggest bed in the town of Ware. Twenty people sleep in it at once! You hope no one snores.

You may travel by ship to the Middle East. Once you arrive, you sleep in a cave until you receive a letter from the local sultan allowing you to pass through his lands. . . . Oh, how you long for the comforts of home!

The pilgrim Saint Ursula (with halo) returns from her trip to the Middle East. This painting was made about 1330. It was displayed in a church in Italy.

Dangers of the Trip

It's weeks later. Your feet are sore. Your money is low. Still you head toward your goal.

What are the risks? Robbers, pirates, and battling armies might attack. Travel is so dangerous that in 1318 some English nuns were not allowed to go on trips. Many went anyway.

Knights form groups to help and protect pilgrims. The Knights of Malta open a hospital. The Templars begin by helping poor pilgrims and end up rich bankers.

This picture shows a pilgrim (in the center) in danger for his soul. The men on either side tempt him to do wrong.

21

The Black Death

The worst danger of the Middle Ages is the Black Death. This sickness, called a **plague**, infected Europe in 1348. More than 25 million people died.

By traveling, you increase your chances of catching the Black Death. It's also harder to move around. Many towns close their gates to you out of fear that you will bring sickness.

However, going to a holy **shrine** might be even more important to you. Like many, you might go there to pray for health.

*A man suffers from the Black Death. The lump on his arm is called a **bubo** and is a symptom of the plague.*

At the Church

You've made it! You crawl up the stairs to the church, praying as you go. Once inside, you kiss the relics and lay thank-you gifts on an altar. If you want to give thanks for a healed arm, you donate a metal arm to the church.

After many prayers, you are given a souvenir. If you are in Jerusalem, it is piece of palm. In Spain, it is a scallop shell. You wear it with pride.

A pilgrim kisses a relic.

Miracles

If you are an important pilgrim, a priest could give you a relic to take home. You can also buy one—if you think it's real. You might use it to try to make miracles.

One pilgrim slipped a piece of a wooden relic under a sick man's pillow as the man slept. The pilgrim claimed that the next morning the man awakened healthy.

An Italian family of the 1400s prays with a holy man.

Pilgrim or Beggar?

In the year 1200, people admired pilgrims. Christians would give you food and a place to stay if you asked. A pilgrim who begged was thought of as a holy person.

Two hundred years later, pilgrims were not welcome in many places. You would break the law if you crossed France on your way to the churches of Rome. King Charles VI of France thought many beggars only pretended to be pilgrims. Many agreed with him.

However, pilgrims did not go away. Today, some still travel to holy places to pray.

A man offers bread to a pilgrim.

Dates to Remember

476	Last Roman emperor overthrown (Romulus Augustulus)
500	Beginning of the Middle Ages
1100s	Inns become common in Europe
1119	Poor Knights of Christ formed (later called the Templars)
1215	A Church council forbids the selling of relics (Fourth Lateran Council)
1285	Eyeglasses invented in Italy
1300	First Catholic Jubilee Year celebrated in Rome
About 1340	Geoffrey Chaucer born
1347	Black Death in Western Europe (accidentally brought by ships from Asia)
1500	End of the Middle Ages

Glossary

bubo (BYOO boh) — a swelling, often found under the arms

Middle Ages (MID ul AY jez) — a time in European history that lasted from the year 500 to 1500

pilgrim (PIL grim) — a person who travels to a holy place for religious reasons

plague (PLAYG) — a widespread and deadly sickness

relic (REL ik) — the body, part of body, or other item related to a holy person

scrip (SKRIP) — a bag or wallet carried by travelers of the Middle Ages

shrine (SHRINE) — a place devoted to a holy person, it often contains a relic or relics

Index

Further Reading

Hinds, Kathryn. *The Cathedral*. Benchmark Books, 2000.

Jordan, William C. (editor). *The Middle Ages: A Watts Guide for Children*. Franklin Watts Incorporated, 2000.

Morris, Neil; John Malam, and Anne McRae. *The Atlas of the Medieval World in Europe*. Peter Bedrick Books, 1999.

Sherrow, Victoria. *Life in a Medieval Monastery*. Lucent, 2001.

Websites to Visit

Middle Ages:
   www.learner.org/exhibits/middleages/

Art of Illuminated Manuscripts of the Middle Ages:
   www.bnf.fr/enluminures/aaccueil.htm

Created by fourth and fifth grade students
   www.kyrene.k12.az.us/schools/brisas/sunda/ma/mahome.htm

About the Author

Melinda Lilly is the author of several children's books. Some of her past jobs have included editing children's books, teaching pre-school, and working as a reporter for *Time* magazine. She is the author of *Around The World With Food & Spices* also from Rourke.